LONDON'S GLORY

TWENTY PAINTINGS OF THE CITY'S
RUINS BY WANDA OSTROWSKA ★ ★ ★
TEXT BY VIOLA G. GARVIN ★ ★ ★ ★ ★

LONDON: GEORGE ALLEN & UNWIN LTD : 1945

Foreword

IN *the spring of* 1942 *the train pulled in as usual to Paddington Station, London. It held its customary quota of troops, Government servants and civilians, of refugees from Hitler's Lands of Nightmare. . . Among the last was a Polish traveller from Lisbon.*

In September, 1939, *Wanda Ostrowska and her family were in the country, as were many of us in England. Skies were blue, the sun constant. It was, you remember, a heavenly, a beneficent month of "mellow fruitfulness". The better for the Germans. We know now, and understand, with what horror Warsaw was visited out of those serene, warm skies, that Canaletto loved to paint. Wanda did not see her home in the capital ruined as it is. She left Poland at once and came through Roumania, Turkey, Syria and Algiers to Marseilles and France. It was a journey both difficult and dangerous, but she made it, like so many other Poles, unhesitatingly. Then, in Paris, during those months of "phoney" war, as we called it over here, she took stock. She was rich in things of the mind and spirit, if in little else. Her family had included connoisseurs of beauty in architecture, sculpture, art and letters. She had lived harmoniously, surrounded by chosen treasures of line, shape, colour and fabric.*

Her problem in Paris was the problem of many people since 1939— *what should the stripped soul do without its trappings? As hundreds of her artistic, intelligent compatriots have done this century past, she got to work and built on inner resources. Madame Ostrowska, who loved painting and poetry, attended art schools in Paris all that bleak winter and in a renewal of study made shift to be happy, though the Nazis were lording it in Warsaw and all that any Pole could do was to go on or go under. She had earlier studied art in Vienna, Heidelberg and other European schools of painting. But experience and Paris pointed and deepened a talent that was by nature and training already true, defined and charming.*

June 1940: *France fell. With the conglomerate rest Wanda, with her husband and children, found their way across beleaguered France to Lisbon and neutral Portugal. Here they breathed anew, took stock again, and Wanda free, in free air, suddenly spread her artist's wings again in earnest. The sun, the air, the sharp lights and shades on the white buildings, her own exquisitely keyed perception of this pure beauty produced lucid and graceful paintings of doorways, façades, houses, churches in the strict southern sun, many of which have found a permanent home in the*

Lisbon Museum, after being exhibited both at Oporto and Lisbon itself. They won a chorus of praise from the critics.

But war went on, relentless, engulfing. Portugal, though lovely, was neutral. Island Britain had become the Noah's Ark of the nations. So Wanda Ostrowska crossed the water to England, and came at last, in the course of her Odyssey, to London. She took rooms, she explored. She saw the bomb damage, the scarred grey streets, the steady faces. She was both enthralled and appalled. Wanda—she is an artist to her finger-tips, as sharply sensitive in soul as in eye—went about amazed, dazed, fascinated. She felt compelled, inspired, to record with brush and pencil what she saw.

She, a stranger, saw our city resting after uttermost conflict. She saw our skeleton buildings, charred wildernesses and lonely spires. She felt with those stones, as though indeed they had breathed and lived. Sometimes she saw a mad and shocking Harlequinade. Sometimes, without knowledge, she peered through the poor ruins and knew the mighty vistas of our history, arcades of triumph and disaster, pediments of solidity...

Bemused, obsessed. . . . This English version of one of her own Polish poems records her feelings better than I can:—

> *"The date? no matter—year? well, '42.*
> *Hours in a train, then London, mighty London*
> *To-day heroic London.*
> *Light here belongs to day,*
> *Night brings but darkness, silence to a city*
> *Crouching in ambush, close indrawn. . .*
> *Because the blows were strong*
> *And fire devouring.*
> *Worst, ah worst*
> *These empty places. . .*
> *Yet from this crumbled house, this toppled street,*
> *This shattered station, shelters underground*
> *People emerged hammered and forged to steel.*
> *Steeled as to heart, steely of eye they beheld*
> *Scattered ruins of churches, stricken museums,*
> *The dead.*
> *They smile, they are kindly, serene:*
> *What was was yesterday,*
> *To-morrow is before them—*
> *To-morrow—and victory".*

Since Mme. Ostrowska wrote this poem, events have sharpened its significance. This summer London was bombed again and she saw for

[6]

herself what she had imagined. Far worse was the complete destruction of Warsaw which was her home. During the nine weeks never-to-be-forgotten battle of the Polish Patriots, most of their capital has been laid in the dust. Here in London we have these ruins and, by the mercy of God, a good deal else. Shattered Warsaw, far away, has nothing.

We were late in keeping our tryst with Poland that September of 1939. To our grief, we could not prevent Warsaw's destruction in 1944. This Polish lady understands our good-will. She sees as we see the permanent in the transitory and offers us these moving pictures of our city as her tribute to London bombed and London not vanquished.

V. G. G.

*Raised small figures in the text
indicate the plate numbers*

DEDICATION

READER, THIS BOOK IS DOUBLE DEDICATED:

OSTROWSKA GREETS OUR WAR-SCARRED LONDON TOWN,

WHERE SHE, WITH MANY POLES, HAS WORKED AND WAITED

FOR A FAIR DAY TO GIVE THEM BACK THEIR OWN.

THEIR OWN WAS WARSAW—WHERE SHE LIVED—AND I

TO PEERLESS WARSAW HEREWITH DEDICATE

MY SHARE OF WORDS THAT, TELLING LONDON'S STORY,

GRIEVE FOR A SISTER CITY'S BITTER FATE,

YET KNOW THAT DUST AND ASHES FLOWER IN GLORY,

AND WARSAW SHATTERED SHALL BE WARSAW GREAT.

OCTOBER: 1944   V. G. G.

LONDON'S GLORY

Twenty Paintings of the City's Ruins

IT must have been in 1834 that Carlyle secured, for a rent of
£35 a year, the lease of that "most massive, roomy, sufficient
old house, with places . . . to hang, say, three dozen hats or
cloaks", and wrote to his Jane a detailed, enthusiastic letter that
cautiously suggested the air of No. 24 Great Cheyne Row,
Chelsea, as "hardly inferior to Craigenputtock".

Chelsea, properly speaking, has nothing to do with this book,
whose twenty pictures honour and record the ordeal of the old
city only. But any great city is compact of lives as well as stones,
and man's mind travels faster than his feet. So that no part of
London is very far, as memory flies, from any other. Huge, old
and sprawling, it lies along its winding Thames like a great lion
couchant: messages, memories, thoughts, experiences, angers,
alarms, denials and acceptances criss-cross along its nerves and
connect its ancient members. Not a citizen that you pin down
for association's sake in one corner but bobs up in another. Not
a citizen's experience in one age that you cannot cap in another.
The centuries seem in fact to dislimn or coalesce, and all
Londoners through the two thousand years of London's certain
existence begin to lose their little place and period and to become
actors on the same stage and players in the same play. It is not
so odd then, is it, that Carlyle's view from that proper London
house, that "right old strong, roomy brick house built nearly
one hundred and fifty years ago and likely to see three races of
these modern fashionables fall before it comes down" should
give a sort of clue into the labyrinthine past of the city, *à la
recherche du temps perdu*. While he was noting down details
of the china room or pantry, of the good floors, the broadish
staircase, the wainscoting and the marble chimney pieces of the
old Stuart house, Carlyle now and again looked out of the
window, and, so he wrote to Jane, said he could "see nothing of
London except by day the summits of St. Paul's Cathedral and
Westminster Abbey, and by night the gleam of the great Babylon affronting the peaceful skies".

Well, it is well over a hundred years now since the sophis-
ticated night-lights of the metropolis shocked our philosopher.

What would he have said if he had looked East and South out of a top-floor window, not very far from his own in Chelsea on September 7th, 1940? It was about six o'clock of a Saturday evening that none of us is likely to forget. The skies seemed peaceful, for it was the end of one of those crisp, golden days with which early autumn can enchant our city. The sun sank in a full splendour of rose and violet, leaving the whole arch of heaven flooded and suffused with lingering radiance. War seemed far away. But the sirens had sounded. The Battle of Britain was in full swing. This is what a diary of those days records:

August 24	First bombs on central London.
August 26	News of 107 raiders down during week-end.
August 26-27	Raiders over London for 6 hours in the night.
August 28-29	Raiders over London for 7 hours.
August 30	63 German raiders down. Intense fighting over London.
September 2	News of 110 German aircraft brought down during the week-end.
September 4	Hitler threatens Britain—"We shall come".
September 5	Mr. Churchill's "grim and gay" speech in the House of Commons.
September 7	Fierce German attacks on the East End and the docks. 103 raiders down.

The docks. As I looked city-wards out of that window, anxious for my friends in Fleet Street who were still at the office, I realised that the after-glow that lingered in the East deepened rather than dimmed, as night came down, and by dark there was no mistaking the sullen, yellowish red of the sky-line behind St. Paul's. Certainly the peaceful skies were affronted, and with gleams. But here was no Babylon, only strong, ancient, ageless, darkened, indomitable, beloved London at bay. Four days later her guns spoke and word went round that the Navy was in the Thames! Whether or no, that was a magic word to Londoners in those hours. On the 15th, the huge delayed-action bomb was got out from under St..Paul's, and driven off and dumped in Hackney Marshes. Everyone took fresh heart. St. Paul's is St. Paul's. We should not have fallen if it had fallen. But that the mighty dome of our Colossus stood helped us petty men to stand.

II. THE CHIMNEY

I use the word "beloved" with intent. It describes the angry, protective, grateful affection that we citizens grew to feel in the nine months' ordeal that followed. One by one, we whose work took us daily to the city saw quiet noble buildings that belonged to our history shattered, wounded, torn and scarred. Great warehouses fell, little houses collapsed like dusty packs of cards. There were strange sights: tea-cups left hanging on a wall, the chain of a lavatory plug dangling stupidly in mid-air, a calendar still standing on a mantelshelf, though fireplace and floor were gone. Once I found a Bechstein grand piano—that instrument of infinite cunning and delight—lying legless and deserted in a roadway. I lifted the lid, but the keys were dead and would not sound. Day by day we got to work as best we could, over broken glass and hose-pipes, across ashes or charred brick. Wonderfully, London Transport got us there, round, over or under "incidents". If not, Shanks's mare served. Shall I ever forget the white, smiling faces of Mrs. Williams and her daughter, our good cleaners at the *Observer* offices in Tudor Street? They lived somewhere down Elephant and Castle way. They were bombed and bombed and bombed. They were so weary that perhaps they would have been glad to be dead—or to miss a day's work. They never missed. They walked to work. All they said was, "Musn't grumble". And "mustn't grumble" was the word of Sergeant Lucas, our faithful commissionaire, and an old soldier from India and the Boer War. On bad days he seemed to improvise coffee out of his hat. As to the messenger boys, the few who were left grew cheekier than ever. How it rained that autumn. How bitter cold and long the winter seemed. Sometimes there was no gas. Sometimes, as at Blackfriars when a main was hit, there was too much. On moonless nights the very air seemed pitch. When the Great Bear swung clear and frosty in the North, or the moon was at full, you could depend upon it that the starred and silvered highways of the sky would be rude and loud with the enemy's monstrous noises. Little things made us happy. Kindness from the grocer, the same familiar faces at the office, your own horizon of roof and chimney unchanged in the morning, the balloons swinging up to their sentinel posts, the steady, English voices of the B.B.C. announcers reading the news at seven and eight o'clock in the morning, pictures in the papers of Mr. Churchill poking about with his stick among the ruins, his smile, under the square

[12]

III. THE BIRDS

bowler hat, if possible grimmer and gayer than before. The papers themselves coming out somehow: delivered somehow. We were all brothers in those days, as perhaps we never were before and never will be again. The City was ours: we were the City. It is something to have known it.

This game of remembering, though, is a dangerous game. Too much has been locked away by all of us these five years past in the chest of memory. I do not know that I would have dared to lift the lid and lean over that chest "in the musk-scented dark of my mind", if the compelling atmosphere of Wanda Ostrowska's paintings had not somehow bidden me do it, and seek among its ghostly contents for a key to their strange quality. There is a last and signal date to recall from that winter of 1940 to 1941, before I slam the lid and lock those memories up again until such time as "emotion, recollected in tranquillity", can make the stuff of fire-side tales—*quand nous serons bien vieille, au soir à la chandelle*, like Ronsard's lady. The diary says, of the last Sunday of the old year:

December 29   Fire sweeps City of London in fierce raid. Guildhall and Trinity House destroyed, and eight Wren churches badly damaged.

It says enough. When we climbed up Ludgate Hill on Monday morning, smoke and steam were still pouring out of what had been Ave Maria Lane and Paternoster Row. A little group of publishers and Evan Pughe of Simpkin Marshalls stood at the corner looking vainly for the places where they had spent their working life. The bitter air—snow was on its way and had fallen already, I think, in the suburbs—was filled with the fumes and atoms of burnt paper, charred wood, dust, rubble and shocked and sooty pigeons wheeling in dismay. St. Paul's stood. But behind the dome, instead of those tall, solid blocks of business houses, there was a single, frail semi-circular screen of wall, with empty windows through which stared a pitiless sky. Inside the Cathedral the lights were lit on the Christmas Tree. But there seemed nothing beyond that screen save desolation—and, indeed, there was in the near neighbourhood very little.

Eighteen months later, by the time Wanda Ostrowska reached London and brought her camp-stool, paint-box and sympathetic Polish eye into these regions, the screen had been pulled down, the shattered fabric of streets and buildings

[14]

IV. THE BRIDGE

cleared. The tide of war had ebbed from these beaches and left the towers, steeples, fragmentary walls, dissected and distorted houses that her pictures show us, standing like lonely signposts in a great wilderness. Pointing to the past, they were both monument and testament. By line and angle, by shape and colour, they told her intuitive heart what they had been and what they had endured. "These stones have heard and shall testify and shall be a memory unto Israel for ever".

* * * * * * *

How long a tale these city ruins had to unfold, what affections and sorrows they have sheltered, what strife beheld, before the immediate past that left them stranded and solitary, each one seemingly alone with the sky and its own thoughts, we shall better understand if we consider Mme. Ostrowska's pictures separately. There are only twenty of them. But if we go about the town with them as guide, visiting, so to speak, her sites and her sitters, we shall find out that she has been led, almost with uncanny instinct (as though some ghostly link-boy had attended her and lighted her through our past), to choose streets, places and buildings not only rich in history but knitted together and interwoven in association through century after century, back through Restoration, Elizabethan, Plantagenet, Norman and Anglo-Saxon London, back to that Londinium itself which Tacitus, though a mere seventeen years had gone by since Claudius and his legions had occupied South-East Britain, spoke of as "thronged with great numbers of merchants and abundance of merchandize". Back to Londinium, which Boadicea and her warriors swept down upon and burnt and sacked in the year A.D. 60, leaving nothing but the red ashes that still lay full fathom five below our London, until the nineteenth century road-makers of Queen Victoria Street and Cannon Street disturbed them, and found underneath the remains of that once flourishing town—metal and glass objects melted all out of shape, burnt bricks, tiles and timber, most strange and moving of all, a huge quantity of wheat, with the form of the grain still distinct though blackened and carbonised by fire. Excavations and finds at different levels prove that several Roman Londons rose above those ashes before, in A.D. 410, the Emperor Honorius's bother with contemporary barbarians forced him to tell the Britons curtly to fend for themselves. None of it seems very far away or unintelligible now.

[16]

V. THE SKULL

Boadicea's devastation may have been the most complete. But sixteen hundred and six years later the Great Fire left such a waste of ravaged acres behind it that Thames was visible from Cheapside. And a mere two hundred and seventy years after that we and our city in our turn have learnt, are still learning, what destruction means.

Roman London tempts one to linger. Bits of Roman walls and causeways, of columns or hypocausts, mosaic pavements, weapons, coins, glass, pottery, leather sandals, combs, hairpins, funeral urns and the like have turned up, some here, some there, under nearly every building that Mme. Ostrowska has painted and under the streets that we shall pass as we follow her about. The huge bronze head of Hadrian, found in the Thames, the line of coins under old London Bridge, the great bronze hand (was it Hadrian's?) that turned up near Lime Street, the altar to Diana, found under Goldsmiths' Hall, the little bronze archer with the silver eyes, found in Queen Street, the green glass Bacchante found in some other of the steep streets running down from the high ground round Leadenhall Street to the ancient Thames wharves of Queenhithe and Billingsgate. Above all, the remains of the villa, with its charming, bright mosaic floor and pillared verandah, that once stood in Bucklersbury and looked across the swift river Walbrook to the Basilica, the Forum, and the painted stucco houses on the other side. . . Such things lay long under London and they set the mind working. I wonder, for instance, if the real reason why these pictures by a stranger to our country are so truly evocative is that the painter, whether by luck or design, has grouped her subjects about four immemorial ideas—church, market, harbour and the law. Pondering that, let us come back to the present and turn into Paternoster Row, off Ludgate Hill, from which point Mme. Ostrowska painted the view in her first picture of St. Paul's lifting its great dome above the red ruins of the Chapter House, in the churchyard, that was finished from Wren's designs in 1712.

*   *   *   *   *   *   *

Nothing is left now of the historic Row, where once the houses of Nelson and Blackwood held the gate. Only the name written up on a white post to mark a track running across a queer weed-grown desert of stone and rubble, for all the world like a sheep track on a high chalk down. All this region,

VI. ENCHANTED CASTLE

Churchyard and Row which, before that, as Stow tells us, was the haunt of bead makers for rosaries, long ago became sacred to books, printers and publishers—part of Stationers' Hall still stands nearby in witness—and so continued down to that ominous Sunday night in 1940. In St. Paul's churchyard, in 1509 after Caxton's death, his apprentice Wynkyn de Worde set up for himself and put out new editions of "Morte d'Arthur" and the "Canterbury Tales". In 1648 appeared "Hesperides" by "a poeticall sonne" of Ben Jonson—otherwise our delightful Herrick—to be sold "at the Crown and Marygold, St. Paul's Churchyard". Here was Addison's coffee-house, where he smoked his pipe and read *The Postman* and kept his ears open for tit-bits for the *Spectator*. Goldsmith knew it, too. Dr. Johnson and Boswell stump up the hill from Fleet Street. "On Friday, April 16, 1781, he carried me to dine at a club, which, at his desire, had been lately formed at the Queen's Arms in St. Paul's Churchyard . . . the company were very sensible and well-behaved men". At the back, No. 50 Paternoster Row, was that Chapter Coffee House from which poor Chatterton wrote bravely to his mother in May, 1770, "I am quite familiar at the Chapter Coffee House and know all the geniuses there". It was still standing in 1856 when Mrs. Gaskell described how Charlotte and Anne Brontë, coming up to London to convince their publishers that they were in fact the authors of "Jane Eyre" and "The Tenant of Wildfell Hall", had stayed here. Why did these young ladies from the country choose a city tavern for their lodging? Because, indeed, they knew no other. It was where their father stayed. Mrs. Gaskell says, "It had the appearance of a dwelling-house two hundred years old or so, such as one sees in country towns; the ceilings of the small rooms were low, and had heavy beams running across them; the walls were wainscoted, breast-high; the stairs were shallow, broad and dark". There was an elderly, grey-haired waiter who still remembered the "quiet simplicity" of the two unexpected ladies who had been guests of the place twelve years before. It sounds, doesn't it, like the city cousin of No. 24, Great Cheyne Row, though dark because of the narrow, bustling street?

As to St. Paul's, he has been standing there in one shape or another since Ethelbert laid his first foundations in A.D. 610 Once, instead of the great dome he now affects, he wore a tall steeple for a hat. That was in his splendid Gothic days, when his stately nave with its twelve bays, his choir windows and his glowing circular East window, put him among the mightiest Cathedrals of Christendom. Very often he lost his steeple and stood there bare-headed, as it were. Lightning struck him, fires burnt him down again and again, tempests knocked the gold crosses off his bell towers. London weather never seems to have been any better than it is now. It didn't make much difference to him. Up he got again with the help of devoted architects and craftsmen and there he is to this day, as though five years' total war were a mere nothing. He and the weather between them caused a lot of trouble and cost the citizens, the Mayor, the Church and the King a pretty penny from first to last. Perhaps that is why from time to time all through the centuries they have been known to treat him rather familiarly. "Paul's Walk", the middle aisle of old St. Paul's, was, to the scandal of poets and divines, a jolly meeting place for most unsacred gossip and affairs. Fops and gallants paraded, your cut-throat bullies back from the wars (there were always wars) swaggered and blus-tered, knaves conspired, hawkers teased you with wares. Look into Dekker and Ben Jonson or into any Elizabethan writer. Even in Chaucer's day they were selling pardons there. Crom-well's men stabled their horses in the nave. Swift would have thought the horse the better company for God and His Saint. And wrathful Dr. Donne, who preached his first sermon as Dean in the Cathedral on Christmas Day, 1621, might have agreed with him. Even in his twenties he was chastening the fools and cheats of Court and City society in the "Satyres". The captain "Bright parcel-gilt with forty dead men's pay", the "velvet justice with a long Great train of bluecoats", the "brisk, perfumed, piert Courtier", the Puritan with his "formal hat", the broker, the bore, the "starving idiot actor" and the rest. . . Shakespeare has them all as clear, but with less scorn. Ben Jon-son said that Donne, for not keeping of accent should be hanged. But it was Donne's heart was out, not his ear.

There it stands, our mighty old cathedral, never quite loved ·in the past as Westminster Abbey was, though our monarchs come with colours, music and procession, riding up the hill to give thanks for victories. Edward III, Henry IV, Henry V, after Crécy, Poictiers, Agincourt, Harfleur; Elizabeth and the Ar-mada; Anne after Malplaquet; Trafalgar; Waterloo. The great names roll on. . . More than once in this war, but more quietly,

VII. PINK TOWER

VIII. ST. VEDAST'S SPIRE, FOSTER LANE

for England stood in greater peril than ever before, King George and Queen Elizabeth have taken the same road for intercession or thanksgiving. Our admirals and generals sleep here. Sir Philip Sidney, Collingwood, Napier, Wellington—and Nelson, and the flags of the *Victory* sleep with him. Wren himself is here, at the heart of his new-built city; Lawrence, Turner and William Blake and Sir Antony Van Dyck. Poets may choose Westminster, but architects and painters are for St. Paul's.

"The glories of our blood and state
Are shadows, not substantial things,
There is no armour against fate,
Death lays his icy hand on kings.
Sceptre and crown
Must tumble down
And in the dust be equal laid
With the poor crooked scythe and spade".

James Shirley's organ music rolls across the little centuries. Paul's still stands alone, aloof above the ruins. He has been and is our care, and we have learned to love him.

* * * * * * *

We must go south towards the river to trace the subject of the next four pictures. And if we cross Ludgate Hill above St. Martin's (which in 1446 was known as "St. Martin in Bowyer-rowe within Ludgate" because it was hereabouts our craftsmen made the long bows and strong bows that won those battles in France and brought us safe out of the Hundred Years' War), and go down by Creed Lane and St. Andrew's Hill, we shall find ourselves where we want to be, and pass a good deal of history as we go by. We shall walk over the site of Baynard's Castle, which was the Tower's opposite number in William the Conqueror's time, to strike awe into the hearts of the far from pacific citizens. They never liked the Tower and they never liked Baynard. It was no heart-break to anyone, when in 1278 the Dominican Friars, who had been housed in Holborn since 1221, received a grant from Edward I of Castle Baynard's lands and moved in, after selling their old property to Henri de Laci, Earl of Lincoln. They seem to have had a more than square deal, for the King ordered the old walls to be pulled down and rebuilt further to the west, outside the Black Friars' precincts. But that was in the hey-day of monasteries, friaries, nunneries,

[24]

IX. FAIRY TALE

and priories. Grayfriars, Whitefriars, Minoresses, Blackfriars, Templars, Hospitallers. . . Their grand buildings stood near the gates all along London Wall. They thronged their streets and left their names to ours. The Dominican buildings ran roughly from Carter Lane to Queen Victoria Street (north to south), and Friar Street to Water Lane (east and west). Printing House Square is very near the Upper Frater or Parliament Chamber where Queen Katharine, on trial for divorce, faced the two cardinals, "the Archbishop of Canterbury, Dr. Warham and all the other bishops" as Cavendish recounts in his "Life of Wolsey". The going was not easy from Henry VIII's point of view. Something about the case stuck in Cardinal Campeggio's throat, as it did in Cardinal Wolsey's and Sir Thomas More's. The Duke of Suffolk stood up angrily "with a stout and hault countenance" for the King. "It was never merry in England", quoth he, "whilst we had cardinals among us". Cardinal Campeggio made answer soberly and the Duke gave over the matter. But the choleric King "was gone into Bridewell at the beginning of the Duke's first words".

Before we cross to Upper Thames Street, shall we recall that years after Henry VIII had dissolved the monasteries and parcelled their lands among his nobles and his creditors, Burbage built the famous "Playhouse" on these grounds. And there exists a deed of conveyance, dated 1612, to prove that Shakespeare, only four years before his death, when most of his worldly interests seem to have been at Stratford, bought a house "abutting upon a streete leading down to Puddle Wharfe, on the east part, right against the King's Majesty's Wardrobe, now or late occupied by William Ireland and erected over a gate leading to a capital messuage". Was he restless for the old player's life in London? Playhouse Yard and Ireland Yard remember him. The house stood near what remains of Wren's Church, St. Andrew's by the Wardrobe. He left it to his daughter Susannah.

Close by is—or was, for only the track is left—Knightrider Street, where once the chivalry of England, as Malory and Froissart knew them, came riding by from the Tower Royal, armed cap-à-pie, with brilliant surcoats and nodding plumes above their visored helmets, steel gauntleted hands, steel-clad bodies, stocky steel-armoured horses. Lances, swords, shields, their ladies' gloves . . . out they rode by Ludgate, up Giltspur

X. LAST AND SORROWFUL

Street to Smithfield, the "Smethefelde" or smooth-field, there to put up their pavilions and joust and tourney until the sun went down. And here, to come back to Henry VIII's time, Thomas Linacre had a house which was haunted by one and all of that serene, enlightened marvellous fellowship of Colet, Fisher, Warham, More, Erasmus and Hans Holbein. Up the hill beside Old 'Change, Dean Colet could see his "Poules' Scole", founded in 1512 for 153 boys. Smelling the dissolution of monasteries long before, he left it to the sturdy Mercers' Company, who saw it safe at last in 1880 to Hammersmith. In the preface he wrote to the Accidence of the Latin Grammar he and his schoolmaster Lily compiled together, he says most beautifully and hopefully:

Wherefore I pray you, all little babes, all little children, learn gladly this little treatise, and commend it gladly to your memories, trusting of this beginning that ye shall proceed and grow to perfect literature, and come at the last to be great clerks. And lift up your little white hands for me which prayeth for you to God, to whom be all honour, and imperial majesty and glory. Amen.

Through the same windows, Erasmus, busy writing to Ammonio, the King's Latin Secretary, once heard horses and asked Linacre to look out and see what was toward. It was Ammonio himself, riding by. "He told me you were just off", wrote Erasmus. "I had a lot to say but another time will do".

And another time must do for other stories about this neighbourhood, for we must hurry past *The Times* office, which inherits many of these departed glories—duly noting that even *The Times* has had a severe hole punched in its face sometime in 1940 or 1941—and go down to Upper Thames Street to look at what is left of "The Wheatsheaf Mills", which Mme. Ostrowska has commemorated in *"The Chimney"*[2] and *"The Birds"*.[3]

* * * * * * *

The gaunt old factory was called the "Wheatsheaf Mills" because of that very chimney that dominates the picture. You will not find it now, nor its haunted-looking interior, which she shows in *The Birds*. It is all pulled down since a lump of loose masonry dropped on some workmen and injured them. Our painter, to tell the truth, had been startled herself. While she was looking about, and watching the birds nesting along the ledges of what once were windows, suddenly, she says, and

XI. PARANOIA

noisily, a piece of wall fell at her feet:
            "The black birds
                Have knocked it off with their wings
                And broken the silence".
    They were rooks, she thinks. Perhaps it was to shake off that
fit of nerves—it was evening, and ruins are not happy places
at dusk—that she went over to the windowed wall and looked
out on to enchantment. Underneath flowed the green water of
the Thames at high tide, slapping along in the black shadow of
the wharves. Overhead the sky was green too, and luminous.
And across the water in this tranquil light sprang the dark,
strong, comforting arch of *"The Bridge"*.[4] Was it Venice? No.
Her chance magic casement opened, not "on the foam Of peril-
ous seas in fairy lands forlorn", but on to London; the City; the
Thames. And the bridge was but our plain, familiar Blackfriars
Bridge, which Cubitt built in the 'sixties.
    The place is not remarkable for history, its spectral beauty
being one of death, not life. Mme. Ostrowska was the last,
perhaps, to give those poor stones a thought. They stood there,
symbol of London's wealth and power through all the ages that
merchants, traders and sailors have been busy about these quays.
The story of the port of London begins up here, where Thames
river runs along by Thames his street and Thames his many
docks and wharves, carrying our fortunes as he has surely
carried them since Cæsar's time, when traders were the only
people great Julius could summon about him in Gaul to tell
anything at all about that annoying white-cliffed island over the
water. Out and away to the seven seas, the countries and the
continents old Thames has carried them, watching the changing
profiles of his ancient city and patiently, with his swans, his
circling sea-gulls, his many water-men, his bridges, beholding
the antic or solemn occasions of his citizens. For they have held
fairs and junketings upon him in such times as the "greate
froste" of December 1683, when, as Evelyn tells us, by New
Year's Day, booths stretched from bank to bank of the river and
fires roared and meat was roasted upon the ice. He has suffered
sad or grave or gorgeous embarkings from the watery stairs
along his banks, of barges carrying princes and prelates, lords
and ladies, Kings, Queens, Lord Mayors, the City Companies
upon their high affairs to palace or prison, when little boats and
wherries crowded round the great boats, "waffeting up and

XII. WHAT FOR

down on Thames", as Cavendish says they did, when, "expecting my lord's departure, supposing to the Tower", they rejoiced when Wolsey's oars made up stream. He heard the Dutch guns in the channel when Dryden and his friends "made haste to shoot the bridge" and dropped down stream to find out what was toward, "seeking noise in the depth of silence". He was the first to hear Handel's silver "Water Music" as King George's pleasure party went up to Richmond. In every age poets and chroniclers have lent him their pen. Hear Dunbar in the fifteenth century:

> Above all ryvers thy Ryver hath renowne,
>> Whose beryall stremys, pleasaunt and preclare,
> Under thy lusty wallys renneth down,
>> Where many a swan doth swymme with wyngis fair;
> Where many a barge doth sail, and row with are,
>> Where many a ship doth rest with toppe-royall.
> O! town of townes, patron and not compare:
> London, thou art the flour of Cities all.

Or Spenser, a hundred years later, with the "bricky towres" of his Epithalamium and its lovely refrain, "Sweet Themmes, run softly till I end my song". Or Herrick shedding his wistful "Tears to Thamasis". Dryden, Gay, Swift, Pope; Wordsworth in 1802 with his morning lines from Westminster Bridge—it was old Westminster Bridge, built in 1739, the first to span Thames after London Bridge itself. Byron, twenty years later, snapping out:

> "A mighty mass of brick, and smoke and shipping,
>> Dirty and dusty, but as wide as eye
> Could reach, with here and there a sail just skipping
>> In sight, then lost amidst the forestry
> Of masts; a wilderness of steeples peeping
>> On tip-toe through their sea-coal canopy;
> A huge dun cupola, like a foolscap crown
>> On a fool's head—and there is London town".

They spake in their times and in their tongues. And, to go back a bit, honest old Drayton made no bones at all about his London,

> ". . . which like a crescent lies
> Whose windows seem to mock the star-befreckled skies";

or about old Thames himself with his "crowded wharfes and people-pestred shores", and

[32]

XIII. CHEERFUL RUINS

"that most costly Bridge that doth him most renowne
By which he clearly puts all other Rivers downe".

The Bridge! that famous London Bridge that Peter de Cole-church finished in 1209, with its many arches, its houses, its chapel, its drawbridge. Costly it was indeed. It was always fall-ing down, as the nursery rhyme tells us, or being burnt, or its foundations were cracked by ice. It was a regular nuisance. People fell off it or were drowned shooting it. Traitors' grisly heads were stuck upon it for all to see. Wat Tyler and Jack Cade marched over it to the certain detriment of city property. All the same it was the citizens' pride, and it stood for six centuries until Rennie built us a new and less eccentric one in 1830. But it was directly responsible for the out-moding of Queenhithe Dock, that antique place of "querns" (mills) and corn, whither we must now address ourselves to find the origin of Mme. Ostrowska's next rather macabre picture, *"The Skull"*[5] It is only a warehouse stripped to the bone, with eyeless windows and roof all awry. It stands at the end of one of the innumerable dark lanes that run down from Thames Street to wharves or river stairs, a little to the right of the old dock. It still looks astonished at what has befallen it, though less grim, as I saw it this summer when willow-herb had pleasantly furnished its upper storeys.

As to Thames Street itself, Upper and Lower, as it runs from our "Wheatsheaf" along past Queenhithe, the Vintry, Three Cranes' Wharf, Dowgate and the Steelyard, under Cannon Street Station to Old Swan Stairs, Fishmongers' Hall, under London Bridge Approach to Billingsgate, the Coal Exchange, the Customs and so to the Tower, there is not a foot of the way that is not dyed in history. The very names you see in the narrow alleys are a jumble of Anglo-Saxon, Norman or Bordeaux or Gascon French, Charter Latin, or Stuart or Cockney English. Sometimes they are what they look, sometimes not. Broken Wharf was "Kayum Fractum" because of two quarrelling abbots in Henry III's time. Fye Foot Lane was "Fyve Foote", Darkhouse and Stew Lane were always that. Queenhithe was "Aetheredeshyd" in Alfred's time, but "Ripa Regina" by the time Edward III let Queen Philippa have the rents. Billingsgate (Belin's Gate), the second oldest dock, displaced it when big ships felt advised to put in below that Bridge and not above it. The Vintry remembers the "marchaunts vintners of Gascoyne,

XIV. LITANY

as well Englishmen as strangers", who in Edward III's time were enjoined to sell Gascoyne wines for 4d. a gallon and Rhenish wines for not more than 6d.! It remembers too, as the whole street does, a wise, shy, comely man in a grey hood who "seemeth elvish by his countenance". For good Dan Chaucer, son of Richard, Vintner, and sometime Clerk of the King's Works and Controller of Customs, was born in this ward. St. Michael Royal, where Lord Mayor Dick Whittington who founded it lies alone, without his cat, remembers La Réole near Bordeaux; Three Cranes' Wharf, the cranes by which the merchants from that very place used to hoist their barrels of wine out of the lighters and sell them there and then. Brickhill Lane in 1440 was the property of one John Birkels. Dowgate, an old water-gate to the Thames, near the mouth of the rushing Walbrook, was "Duuegate" and belonged to the men of Rouen, under Edward the Confessor. The Steelyard belonged to merchants of the Hanseatic League from Henry II's time and to German merchants as far back as Ethelred's (A.D. 978). They were rich and powerful and caused great heart-burnings among home-born merchants and 'prentices. Elizabeth turned them out in 1598. So it goes on. . . Duck's Foot Lane was the Duke of Suffolk's Foot Lane to Thames. Billingsgate was not always solely consecrated to fish, though excavations for Cannon Street, discovering a stack of Roman-ancient oyster shells seven foot thick, suggest it was always a fishy district, and monk Fitzstephen knew his "fyssheful river of Thames". Come along now to Pudding Lane, where the Great Fire started on the night of Sunday, September 2, 1666, and as we climb up to that same Eastcheap to find St. Margaret Pattens, whose tall lead spire points sky-wards out of the pile of Mme. Ostrowska's *Enchanted Castle*,[6] let us consider how this church, and St. Mildred's, Bread Street, which is *"Pink Tower"*[7] and *"St. Vedast, Foster Lane"*[8] St. Alban, Wood Street, which gave her *"Fairy Tale"*[9] and *"Last and Sorrowful"*,[10] lovely St. Mary-le-Bow, are all children of Wren, and rose up after the greedy flames had raged over three-quarters of the city, devouring palaces, halls, churches, houses, gardens and with them, so it seems, the seeds of the Plague that only the year before had emptied London of life and filled it with corpses, coffins, pits, fear, the dreadful sign on the door, the dreadful bell. It is all set down by that good Londoner, Daniel Defoe, in "The Journal of the

XV . EMPTINESS I

Plague Year". As for the fire, Evelyn and Pepys read now as though they had been with us in 1940.

* * * * * * *

Margaret, Mildred, Vedast, Alban and Mary-le-Bow . . . the very names are like a bell to toll us back to their sole selves. Every one has a long history before the Fire that made them phœnixes. St. Margaret Pattens stands on the corner of Rood Lane and Eastcheap and has so stood since 1067. You cannot see the pleasant old-fashioned façade in the picture. The church stands squarely towards the busy pavements, and Mme. Ostrowska has painted only the slender spire rising above a stricken block of shops and offices, as she saw it from the corner of the next turning, Mincing Lane. It was "so called because of olde time pattens were there usually made and sold". There was a family called Patin living close by in the twelfth century. But their name surely came from their calling, which was to make those necessary wooden clogs which got our London dames through the worst of the mud and filth. Good housewives "safe through the wet on clinking pattens tread", says Gay. For St. Mildred's we must go westwards along Eastcheap and Cannon Street (Candlewick Street that was) to its junction with Friday Street—not forgetting as we cross King William Street to salute the ghosts of Falstaff and the Boar's Head Tavern, and Goldsmith's "Reverie" on the same. Poor and hungry, he worked at a chemist's nearby when first he came to London. From here you will see, as our painter saw, the lonely, square red-brick tower, which is all that is left to tell us of "St. Mildrid in Bredstrate", whose church has stood here since 1223 at least in honour of the saintly daughter of Merwald of Mercia who was first Abbess of Minster. Here Shelley married Mary Godwin on the last day of December in 1816, the year which had seen so many tragedies. All that is left now is the tower. I saw it in a fierce windy sunset, "burst open like a rose", like the mast of Flecker's ship. Turn up Cheapside and west again for Foster Lane and St. Vedast. You can see very well where you are going, for the houses that lined the old streets are melted into air, into thin air. Both church and lane are called after good St. Vedast (or Vast) of Arras who left his name to the cathedral of his own city, as well to this one foundation in London. In 1128 "Seint Vastes lane qui ducit versus Aldridesgate" already had its church "Sancti Vedasti". Golden Herrick, son of a gold-

[38]

XVI. EMPTINESS 2

smith and born in Wood Street, Cheapside, home of gold-smiths, was baptized here on August 2nd, 1591. For St. Alban you must continue up Noble Street and Monkwell Street into Hart Street, where roofless old St. Giles stands by a large chunk of Wall—that same wall that the Romans put up and took along the site of what is still called London Wall and from which, if you look southwards down Wood Street towards Words-worth's plane tree, you will see what is left of venerable St. Alban standing at what was the corner of Little Love Lane. This is the eldest of all these elderly parish churches, for the Saint himself was the first English martyr; and when King Adelstane put up this church to him in A.D. 930, he righteously broke up Roman bricks to build it. Some accounts say that King Offa, who died in A.D. 796, had a chapel here nearly two centuries earlier. But one story does not invalidate the other. In the chill and timeless evening gleam the tall Gothic colonnades seem fallen with some Merlin trick about them. They looked, thought Mme. Ostrowska, like the enchanted castle of a for-gotten beauty, sleeping there these three hundred years. Were she to wish . . . would a Glass Mountain appear at the end of the street?

By contrast, on a halcyon day of little breezes and soft sun-shine, when she came upon St. Mary-le-Bow in Cheapside, she found the pale and sorrowful beauty of the springing tower and steeple, with its bows, or arcs, or arches, less credible than her twilight fantasies. What had this forlorn nobility to do, under the clear blue, with the ugly madness of the crippled houses close by? She gives us one of these, by the way—it is "*Para-noia*"[11]. St. Mary of Bow Bells, St. Mary of the Arches, "St. Marie de Arcubus", "Nostre Dame des Arches", "Our Lady of the Bowe". . . . She goes back a long way, to the Conqueror, Stow says. Her Norman crypt has survived the work of the would-be Conqueror of to-day. The bells that made Whitting-ton turn again, and rang the curfew when Edward III was King, perished, with the church itself, in the Great Fire. Now the later ones of 1758 are smashed and silenced, too. And the famous tower? Christopher Wren, coming to rebuild, and excavating for foundations, found, 18 feet under the Norman crypt, a Roman causeway, 4 foot thick. "He then concluded to lay the foundation of the Tower upon the very Roman causeway as most proper to bear what he had designed, a weighty and lofty

XVII. PARROTS

structure". Truly it has borne that tower, the tower of a large-hearted, gracious church, which, with its rights of sanctuary, harboured rogues and knaves and the persecuted as generously as good men and true. She was the chief church of Cheapside, that great market of old time, with all its little markets running out of it like tributaries, the place of poets and 'prentices, of guilds and craftsmen, where once the Great Conduit and the Little Conduit provided sweet fresh water for the citizens (and "red and white wine to drink for all such as wished" on feast days or fair days), and where Daniel Defoe stood in the pillory and many another poor sinner sat in the stocks. To ring us in to this vivid world of Chepe, listen to the jolly rhymes the boisterous 'prentices and the bell-ringer exchanged in curfew days:

"Clerke of the Bow Bell, with the yellow lockes,
    For thy late ringing thy head shall have knocks".
"Children of Cheape, hold you all still,
    For you shall have the Bow Bell rung at your will".

*   *   *   *   *   *   *

St. Mary-le-Bow stands in the middle of Chepe. But properly speaking, she belongs to Cordwainer Ward. Of the seven great parish churches that once opened their doors to the merchants and sober families of Cheapside Ward, not one is left. The last to go was St. Lawrence Jewry by Guildhall, the richest of Wren's churches and as justly proud of its incomparable Grinling Gibbons panellings and wreathed carvings as of its great Renatus Harris organ. The same raid, that of December 29, 1940, brought down Guildhall itself, which was an insult to the City's pride, though the fifteenth century walls—the oldest part of the historic hall—stood up to bombing as they had to the Fire. Gog and Magog fell with the Hall they guarded. Their giant ghosts must be growling *"What For?"*[12] as helplessly as Mme. Ostrowska when she painted the picture of that name, which is a view of Guildhall's and St. Mary-le-Bow's remains seen from Love Lane. The banquets of my Lord Mayor, his sheriffs, aldermen, the City fathers and their honoured guests were held here since 1501. In Edward III's time it was "The Hall of the Pleas of the City". The worshipful grandeur of the old place has for so long been inseparable from the name and affairs of London that it is queer to hear Stow talking about its predecessor before 1400—"a little old cottage in Alderman-burie", where payment of "gild" was made.

[42]

XVIII. ROMAN RUINS

All round Guildhall were scattered the noble Halls of the City Companies. Most have met mortality, like Haberdashers' Hall, to whose ruins, though, a Harlequin sun was kind when Mme. Ostrowska sat in Gresham Street and painted them as "*Cheerful Ruins*"[13]. Colour played hide-and-seek there, that day, though you cannot see it in the reproduction. Orange, pink, black, purple, scarlet, lizard-green and cinnabar peeped out, she says, and vanished as the conjuring rays danced out and in. It was a pretty chance, for the old company of Hurrers—as the Haberdashers were called when Henry VI incorporated them, though they were a "mistery" long before that—included "Cappers and Hat Marchantes", and when you think of the warm velvets, the gold and pearls, the lawns and linens, felts, feathers, beavers and furs that have gone to the making of our headgear down the ages, it seems, doesn't it, as though the gay and glittering scraps and snippets were lying there among the old stones. The Haberdashers were eighth in the ranks of the twelve great Livery Companies who numbered also the Mercers, the Grocers, the Drapers, the Fishmongers, the Skinners, the Merchant Taylors, the Ironmongers, the Vintners, the Clothmakers and, of course, the Goldsmiths. And before we let that rich and powerful name carry us back to Chepe, let us spare a thought for one of the humble companies—like the Watermen, they have no livery— whose little hall in Silver Street is gone. The company was the Worshipful Company of Parish Clerks. Stow says: "The Parish Clarkes in London of olde time were accustomed yearly to assemble and to play some large historie of Holy Scripture", such as the three days' cycle of the "Passion of Our Lord and the Creation of the World", which they gave in 1390 before Richard II, his Queen, Court and no doubt enraptured subjects. For when has a Londoner not loved a show or a play? Nearer our own time, James Bone, who has an eye like Lamb's own for the odd and the moving, tells us they "convene in a little old hall in Silver Street and dine round a large, queer table shaped like a bass viol, and probably sing glees and catches" until the candles are snuffed and the moon goes down. It was from Silver Street—Selvernestrate of old time—"I think of silversmiths dwelling there", that Mme. Ostrowska, looking over her shoulder, saw the dome of St. Paul's again, rising unconquerable behind wrecked façades and mutilated walls. They chilled her blood. The picture called "*Litany*"[14] records what she saw and felt.

[44]

XIX. EVENING

If silversmiths lived in Silver Street and, as they and the gold-smiths and jewellers and some ironmongers did, in Wood Street, Bread Street, Foster Lane and Noble Street—where also were timber merchants and bakers, as there were milkmen in Milk Street, fishmongers in Friday Street and vendors of honey in Honey Lane—the home of metal-workers and money makers and changers was in "Westceape" (the same Chepe), which had been the heart and nerve centre of London's trades and markets since the Conqueror's time, perhaps before. For tradition persists more obstinately in London than anywhere else in the world. The goldsmiths' quarter was called "Orfaveria" in Henry III's time—it ran from Wood Street to Foster Lane—"Aurifabria" in the first Edward's. By the time Herrick was born, it was "Goldsmiths' Row", and Stow called it "the most beautiful frame of Fayre houses and shoppes in London or elsewhere, built by Thomas Wood, sheriff and goldsmith, in 1491". In 1622 it was "the glory and beauty of Cheapside", and well it might be, since in 1594 it had been new "painted and gilt". The goldsmiths were forerunners of the great banking companies, and in 1327 gold and silver might be sold only here, or at the King's Exchange—Old 'Change which used to run down to St. Augustine's Church, outside St. Paul's eastern boundary. The old life of this quarter of Chepe, where the craftsmen were cheek by jowl with the tradesmen, and life was communal and ruly, in spite of the unruly 'prentices, reminds one of nothing so much as "The Meistersingers of Nüremberg". For here, too, we had our singers, our poets, our playwrights, our excellent discoursers in prose. Herrick, son of a goldsmith, was born in Wood Street; Sir Thomas More in Milk Street; John Donne, son of an ironmonger, in Bread Street. Shakespeare in 1604 lodged with Christopher Mountjoy, "a tire-maker whom he had known for the space of tenne years", at a corner of Monkwell Street. Do not forget Spenser born in East Smithfield, and Keats on Finsbury Pavement, Ben Jonson, son of a bricklayer, Chaucer in the Vintry, and too many others to name, but greatest of all, John Milton, son of a scrivener, born at the sign of the Spread Eagle in Bread Street, and a Londoner all his days, except for those spells at Cambridge, Horton and abroad. Do not forget that "The Mermaid" itself, that marvellous tavern of wit and story, stood in Cheapside between Friday Street and Bread Street. Beaumont gives it immortally:

[46]

XX. ST. BRIDE'S STEEPLE

What things have we seen
Done at the Mermaid! heard words that have been
So nimble, and so full of subtile flame
As if that everyone from whence they came
Had meant to put his whole wit in a jest,
And had resolved to live a fool the rest
Of his dull life;

And old Thomas Fuller, who was only eight when Shakespeare died, but must have had his baby ears enchanted with tales of those great men, takes us straight indoors:

"Many were the wit combats betwixt Shakspere and Ben Jonson, which two I beheld like a Spanish galleon and an English man-of-war; Master Jonson, like the former, was built far higher in learning; solid but slow in his performances. Shakspere with the English man-of-war, lesser in bulk, but lighter in sailing, could turn with all tides, tack about, and take advantage of all winds by the quickness of his wit and invention".

* * * * * · * *

Before we go west out of Cheapside, along Newgate Street, out of the invisible ancient New Gate, that was even new in Roman times, we must just step north a little to wonder and grieve at two strange panoramas—which Mme. Ostrowska simply calls "*Emptiness I*"[15] and "*Emptiness II*".[16] The first is a view from Whitecross Street of ancient St. Giles, where Martin Frobisher and John Foxe are buried, as well as Milton, and where Oliver Cromwell, aged 21, married Elizabeth Bourchier, a city merchant's daughter, on 22 August, 1620. St. Paul's dome peers over the horizon. The second is a northerly view from Jewin Street, looking from the old Jewish Garden and Burial Ground over to Barbican to where Bridgewater House once stood, rather to our left. Yes, Bridgewater House which used to know the voices of Lord Brackley, Mr. Thomas Egerton, and the Lady Alice Egerton for whose grave, delightful youth John Milton penned his "Comus". And here, on the verge of chaos, let us recapture a memory of that tremendous master who, as Dryden thought, "cuts us all out and the ancients too". In 1646 he lived at No. 17 Barbican and taught school. In 1662, he married his third wife, "a gentle person of a peacefull and agreeable humour" from this very Jewin Street, whence he soon removed to Artillery Walk, Bunhill Fields, there to spend his last years.

By this time he was blind. And nothing is stranger in this fugue of London's story than the thought of the old, blind poet, writing and musing up here, just out of reach of the terrible Fire, while down by the river dear and human Samuel Pepys was bustling from Seething Lane to the Tower, from White-hall to Thames Street, and over the water to a little ale-house in Bankside "and there staid till it was dark almost and saw the fire grow and as it grew darker, appeared more and more, and in corners and upon steeples, and between churches and houses, as far as we could see up the hill of the city, in a most horrid malicious bloody flame, not like the fine flame of an ordinary fire . . . we saw the fire as only one entire arch of fire from this to the other side the bridge, and in a bow up the hill for an arch of above a mile long: it made me weep to see it". In his solitude the poet up the hill must have heard the roar and crack of falling timber, and the distracted people crying and lamenting. Next year "Paradise Lost" was published. In truth he had seen "no light, but rather darkness visible".

    *   *   *   *   *   *   *

Well, time is short now, night is coming on, and we have been a long way. Going down Newgate Street, past Ivy Lane, from which, as you will see by " *Parrots*"[17], the shreds of houses beyond Paternoster Row look, to a reticent imagination, almost shockingly exposed, do we in the half-light encounter the shade of young Coleridge "wildly rushing through Newgate to be in time for school, when he upset an old woman's apple stall" and "Oh, you little devil" she exclaimed as the apples rolled in the gutter, and "Oh, you little angel!" as he picked them up. Or perhaps "the good old relative (in whom love for-bade pride)" is hastening home from that same school with the precious basket emptied now of its "viands" and "more tempting griskins", which that "poor, friendless boy", Charles Lamb, has certainly devoured, his hunger "breaking down the stony fences of shame and awkwardness". Of course the school is Christ's Hospital. But the tale of the fellowship of the Blue-coat boys, with their ruffs and yellow stockings and long gowns which they have worn since the boy King Edward VI endowed them and their school on the site of the old Franciscan Monastery, is too long to be told here. Close by Ivy Lane was one of Lamb's favourite taverns, the "Salutation and Cat" of merry name and merry memory. I would rather think of it than of "the

Shambles" Newgate once was, when butchers used it and it stank powerfully. I would rather think of it than of the grim old prison, whose nightmarish past no charms of "The Beggars' Opera" can defeat, and going past the site of which, on the corner of Old Bailey, we hurry our steps a little towards the solid, unghostly viaduct. Let it swing us clear over to Holborn, across the sharp descent and muddy valley that caused trouble for labouring man and beast for centuries until the viaduct spanned it and spanned a wealth of history, too, in 1869 at a cost of two million sterling. Bunyan knew well enough what the ascent was. If anyone knew the Hill Difficulty it was he. He died at the top, at the sign of the star on Snow Hill, which used to climb up, narrow, steep and slippery from Holborn Bridge:

"Taking a tedious journey in a slabby, rainy day, and return-
ing late to London, he was entertained by one Mr. Strudwick,
a grocer on Snow Hill, with all kind endearments of a loving
friend, but soon found himself indisposed with a kind of
shaking, as it were an ague, which increasing to a kind of
fever, he took to his bed, where, growing worse, he found that
he had not long to last in this world, and therefore prepared
himself for another, towards which he had been journeying as
a PILGRIM and Stranger upon earth the prime of his days".

And narrow, steep and slippery Breakneck stairs climbed down to Fleet Market and Seacoal Lane and Green Arbor Court, where poor Goldsmith lodged.

Bunyan died in 1688, but Malcolm Letts, whose grandfather had a house, now annihilated, in Bartlett's Buildings, Holborn, in the "Passage" of which Charles and Mary Lamb went to school, remembers that even in Victorian days Holborn Hill was reckoned a heavy hill; "spare horses were kept standing at the bottom to help buses and waggons up the incline, and at the top of the hill on each side were men with drags to place under the wheels of the carts and buses as they descended". The reason of all this was that other nuisance and headache to London citizens, the Fleet river, more rudely the Fleet Ditch, which, by the time it reached Holborn Bridge was called the Holebourne, when it wasn't alluded to as Turnmill brook. Once it flowed sparkling and useful down from the many springs in Hampstead and Highgate, through Hockley in the Hole and Saffron Hill, and broadly out to the broad Thames, between Blackfriars and Bridewell. Once, ships sailed up it and anchored by Holborn Bridge. Once, Holborn was only one of its four bridges—Bridewell, Fleet Street, Fleet Lane were the others. Roman coins have been found in its bed. But like the Walbrook its course, through the years, was choked with filth and refuse. Plaintive orders from court and city to the citizens to clean it crop up all through the records. Now and again they tried, and then forgot about it again. Wren had a shot at it after the Fire, and his New Canal with its broad wharves and brave market did indeed last nearly a hundred years. But in 1764— four years after the old walls and gates of the city were finally pulled down—everyone's patience seems to have run out. They arched the river over and imprisoned it in the sewer that runs under Farringdon Street and New Bridge Street. It had its day and gave a name to that other river of news on its western bank.

As to Holborn—it was a prebendal manor of St. Paul's, outside the city boundaries, and comprised the lands of the Bishop of Ely and of the Black Friars and Templars, before these orders moved down to the Thames, where we have already met them. Mme. Ostrowska, for her next picture *"Roman Ruins"*[18], an impression of the accidentally classic remains of the City Temple from the juncture of Shoe Lane and Charterhouse Street below Holborn Viaduct, did not go so far west as Ely Place or Lincoln's Inn, where gardens of roses and strawberries flourished long ago. In the thirteenth century, after the Dominicans had gone, Henri de Laci, that Earl of Lincoln who lies up the hill in St. Paul's, cultivated apples, pears, "large nuts" (perhaps walnuts), and cherries, beans, onions, garlic, hemp and sorrel, besides grapes, salads, roses, lilies, violets, herbs and the like. Not only did he supply his own groaning tables. He made at least £130 in our money by marketing his surplus. More than one patch of earth in London city, churned up by bombs and sheltered by ruined walls, has produced vegetables and flowers in our time. But as she crossed to Thavies Inn, which was once an Inn of Chancery pertaining to Lincoln's Inn, where Dr. Donne, in company with other gay and restless wits, studied for six months of his stormy, brilliant youth, she caught a glimpse of the Memorial Hall in Farringdon Street. It stands where the Fleet Prison stood and is not beautiful, except across the ruins and in the dying light that made her call the picture *"Evening"*[19].

Evening it is, as we go the last few steps with her, past the skeleton of St. Andrew's, Holborn, where Hazlitt married

Sarah Stoddart, and who should be best man and bridesmaid but Charles and Mary Lamb, no doubt in snuff-coloured coat and the best China silk. Stand here in Farringdon Street, across the road and a little short of the Hall. Look up, across the torn and tattered walls, the shabby blocks, the sturdy, faithful traffic of bus, waggon, lorry, van, taxi and man going about his affairs—traffic which neither Hitler's threats nor his Luftwaffe could ever stop or greatly disturb. You see that steeple? It is St. Bride's—and look how:

". . . her aery, unsubstantial charm
   Through flight on flight of springing, soaring stone
   Laughs into life full mooded and fresh-blown";

St. Bride's, Wren's tallest steeple, out-topping even St. Mary-le-Bow and out-soaring in very truth the shadow of our night. Milton lived in her churchyard with one "John Russell, a taylour"; Dryden in 1673 was not far away in Salisbury Court; Samuel Richardson, whose life was linked with Stationers' Hall up on the hill, lies buried here; and so does Wynkyn de Worde and so does Sackville the poet, and gallant, rare, passionate Lovelace. Our wheel has come full circle. Shall we pause to consider Bridewell that was a palace before it became that hideous house of correction named, as the church is, after St. Brigit's well that bubbled fresh, clear and healing, as once so many wells in London did? Shall we stop to recall the rascals who haunted here, as they did at Whitefriars and Blackfriars and wherever holy sanctuary degenerated into licence? No. It is not the City's sores, but the wounds and scars in a noble fabric that Mme. Ostrowska, our friend from Poland, commemorates. Ugliness and pain, she found, vanished from London:

   . . . when evening mist clothes the riverside with poetry, as with a veil, and the poor buildings lose themselves in the dim sky, and the tall chimneys become campanile, and the warehouses are palaces in the night, and the whole city hangs in the heavens, and fairyland is before us. . .

So another painter, Whistler, wrote. And, he went on, at that blue and shadowy moment, "the wayfarer hastens home. . ." Thither must we, too, hasten, leaving the voices of poets and people still talking softly across the years, leaving the great dome and the lapping river, and the pointing spires among their ruins, dreaming on things to come.   V. G. G.

LIST OF PLATES

LIST OF PLATES